The Merry Dance

Raymond Evans was born in industrial South-East Wales in 1944, a few months before the D-Day landings and migrated with his parents to Australia in 1948–49. He is best known as an Australian social historian, widely published in such fields as race relations, convict studies, war and society study, gender relations and popular culture. His writings include *Exclusion, Exploitation and Extermination*, *Loyalty and Disloyalty*, *The Red Flag Riots*, *Gender Relations in Australia*, *1901: Our Future's Past*, *Fighting Words*, *Radical Brisbane* and *A History of Queensland*. This volume is his second collection of poetry.

Also by Raymond Evans and published by Ginninderra Press
Half Century

Raymond Evans
The Merry Dance
Poems of Memory and Imagination

'If I can't dance, I don't want to be part of your revolution.'
Emma Goldman (1869–1940)
(attributed)

The Merry Dance: Poems of Memory and Imagination
ISBN 978 1 76041 806 9
Copyright © Raymond Evans 2019

First published 2019 by
GINNINDERRA PRESS
PO Box 3461 Port Adelaide 5015 Australia
www.ginninderrapress.com.au

Contents

Cold Comfort	7
Getting There	8
Holiday (1955)	9
Hireith (for St David's Day)	11
Welsh Christmas (1947)	16
Brisbane (1949)	20
Initiation	22
Matinee	24
The Explorer	25
Westerlies (A Rubaiyat)	28
Another Sunday	29
The Vow	30
Saturday Night	33
Foolish Nightmare	36
Transition	37
Here We Go Round the Sun	40
Ooh Ma Soul!	41
Premeditated Siege	44
Brisbane (2017)	45
Contemplation before Annihilation	48
Lenore (1964)	50
New Find	53
Dawn Service	54
Vietnam Days	56
All the Way (1966)	59
Memory	69
Epiphany	71
Civilisation	76
Lost Nights	77
1788 and All That	80

Brisbane (1861)	84
War Correspondent	88
Missing in Action (1918)	92
Deliverance	94
Frontier (1868)	95
Imagination	99
Intercourse	101
The Visit	104
Uncatalogued Nightmare	106
Rain Dance	107
Separate Tables	109
Mother	111
Passing Through	115
Gifts	118
Chinese High Noon	120
Requiem	122
'Dream On'	123
Last Night	125
Haiku	127
Dilemma	128
September 2001	130
Life (2017)	133
Sonnet for Seventy-four	136
Evening Coming On	137
Some Conclusions	138
The Future	139
Last Dance	140

Cold Comfort

The white rib of sand
in my back pocket
is all I have left
of the summer.

Crows rasp and chatter.
They wield and scatter
in marbled skies.
The wind picks up again.

The days are folding in.

A sickle moon
glimmers like chrome.

The sand in my pocket
is cold and old.

Getting There

Nothing much of a platform, and nobody but holidaymakers,
bunched like dark grapes on either side,
eager for the bus and the beach,
the bumpy expedition down to the sea,
glistening through troughs and foam. Passengers
impatient to be off from a drab inland
to the smack of bright air and a catch of
salt in the nostrils. The insect whirr about us
soporific in the glazed afternoon light.

Beside me, Dad, marshalling the luggage –
warm-brown and familiar from past adventures.
This confusion of voices and a boiled egg
taste in my mouth, salted with the
admonition to 'not get bits of shell on the
seat' of a grubby train, still labouring
out of last century into Landsborough.
The attendants, slow as sleepwalkers, stuffing
the old bus's bowels with our hillock of paraphernalia.

Eventually, this stuttering impulse towards the coast,
as the antique vehicle coughs and complains
over its barren track. Then rollicking downhill,
its sides jolting in merriment as if unhinged
as we crane our necks, my cousin and I,
jockeying for first glimpse of the ocean, as if rising
for some unexpected prize to audience acclaim:
a preposterous garland of gold, tracing a shoreline
of green confusion and some chance, at last, of joy.

Holiday (1955)

The sheets
so perfectly white I remember
and so crisply starched –
tucked in so tight.
My little feet
going 'snicker-snack',
almost 'running on the spot'
sideways across and within them,
feeling their cool thrill
against my shins and toes,
as, faintly, though distinctly
to my ears,
the sloughing surf,
crashing and sighing interminably
on gleaming sands
in waiting out there
at the far end of Bulcock Street.

Inside my body,
diving like a dolphin
into that encompassing deep,
a dreamy excitement swirling:
a small ecstasy
in that encircling moment –
The worries and fears
of school and growing up
behind and before me
obliterated and lost
in the creamy caress of those sheets;
the majesty of the calling waves.

I lay there,
clutching alertness,
my erstwhile companion,
eager to leave
on that first night
of long beach days,
stretching away
into an azured distance,
as the dreams rolled in
like tumbling waves
and carried me off
into a shining morning –
so blue and yellow and sandy-white
with the mad gulls crying,
sandpipers wading
past castles and shells;
and the vast soldier-crab battalions
retreating in tides of precision
before my eager, running feet.

Hireith (for St David's Day)

In Fifties Australia
daffodils meant 'Home' –
'the Old Country' as we called it
(though the new one
was much older).

Wales from afar
shone solid and golden
as the British sovereign
pressed at birth
into my hand;
or those parcels of treasure
arriving as regular saviours
from flat, local commonality:
Beano and *Dandy*,
Swift and *Topper*,
Sunny Stories, Quality Street
and Smarties.

Wales was
my mother's Welsh cakes
(a recipe she'd never disclose);
blue aerogrammes appearing weekly
in the tin letter box;
the smell of black pudding
sizzling in the pan;
my father singing 'Sospan Fach'
in the bath
(and not standing
for the National Anthem).

It was plump and round
like the white Sealyham,
Betty,
waiting obediently
with smiling jaws
on Nan's doorstep,
her black claws dancing
a fast click-clack on the stone;
her paws never stepping down
to the pavement
as I run to hug her.

And being carried by my dad
into the darker swaths
of Cwm Woods,
away from the colliery,
the summer sun dappling down
through thick, oaken branches;
acorns on the ground,
squirrels running,
everything a swirl of green and red
as he spins me round,
around and around,
in the leafy silence.

And that day,
gazing down from my stroller
and there
amidst the grey slag
from the tip
and a snatch of wild grass,
that lost badge,
a shiny mulberry and black,
reading *Mickey Mouse Chums,*
with his 1940s face
(that seemed so Welsh to me),
smiling like Betty's,
grinning up a welcome
as Dad affixed it to my Burberry,
wondering aloud
at his boy's keen awareness.

Blazing fires
and the press of stale bodies;
drab clothing,
laughter and singing
as I performed
'Mr Shinotski' for them,
my wooden barrow
that Granddad made me
heavy with books and toys.

And when, at last,
as we left for good,
how I kissed all goodbye
except aged Bopah,
with her ghostly skin
of talcum and tissue
and her toothless mouth,
a daunting cave.

We went and the door closed.
But knowing myself wrong,
turned and ran back;
burst into the room
to where she sat in a far corner,
kissing her full
on her ancient lips,
her face so close,
eyes welling with tears.

'Darling boy,' she whispered
in my ear.
'Darling boy.'

And so we left South Wales
and Great Britain behind
as my father carried me
up a swaying gangplank
with dark Indians all around;
and looking back once
at the spire
of the Liverpool clock tower,
reading seven p.m.
through swirling fog.

Such little things remembered.
Such little things.

Welsh Christmas (1947)

My eyes
slowly rise
with the rising damp
up the yellowed walls
to the faint line
where the low ceiling meets.

Listening so hard
my eyeballs ache.
Warm and small
under the crimson eiderdown.

Away in the dark,
thunder beckons:
Father Christmas – *Sion Corn* –
is coming.

Lying here
in the old bed
at 6 Court Street,
my father sings to me,
his strong body beside me,
propped on one elbow:

There's a long, long trail a'winding
into the land of my dreams…

And

I'm sending a letter to Santa Claus.
A letter I hope he receives…

My mother's dark stocking
hangs limp over the fireplace.

He sings
every song he knows.
(He has the best voice in Wales.)
But my eyes are glued open.
My heart won't stop dancing,
as, defeated,
he rises
(along with the rising damp)
to leave.

He disappears down
the crooked stairway
and I am across that room,
reaching through the bannisters
on my belly
to grab him
by his one tuft of hair
as the shiny head bobs past.

He hangs
like a Christmas bauble
in mid-stride…

Then, miraculously,
I am waking
with the dark stocking
beside me,
bulging like a digesting python:
Out comes
a tiny polar bear,
rearing up,
metal arms out-stretched;
a new Mr Buffin book
about his *cat*!
Tangerines and walnuts
in the shell;
and right down in the toe,
an oval squeaker,
shiny plum-purple,
with Pluto's face,
grinning up at me,
winking almost…

Why do I remember
this moment
with uncommon clarity?
Is it just
Pluto's beaming presence?
Or is it my parents,
their bodies scooped
around me
and my presents,
urging me on
in low, conspiratorial tones
to fresh delights
on the rumpled bed,
as the snow falls gently outside.

Brisbane (1949)

We came in summer:
The heat
a hard slap to the face
as we climbed from the cabin.
The deck awash with light,
drenched and shimmering,
assaulting the eyes.
A smell in the air –
rot and peach combined.
A taste like metal
on the tongue.
No whisper of a breeze.
Insects dancing in harsh sunshine.

Was I still aboard
or down on the dock
when a stuffed koala
was thrust at me?

Red and green slashes of poinsettia
on the stark dress
of the woman
bending over me,
large-breasted
and drawling something;
Indian-dark skin.
A splash of sweat
spreading from each arm-pit…

Auntie Dot…

And my cousin Harvey,
freckled and shy
in an olive pith helmet,
like Stanley meeting Livingstone –
inches shorter than me,
inching towards me,
saying nothing,
proffering the koala.

I am not used to this.

Initiation

My feet know this soil's essence:
its rough declensions –
the heft of it;
its slope and bend.
Grass soured like tobacco stain,
clenched to the packed earth,
storing in heat like a kiln.

They would cross with splayed feet,
confident on shale and gravel;
run along tree branches
with gripping toes
like anthropoids.
I yearn to blend,
longing to be home here –
but the tough hide of this land shrugged,
flinched and crackled at my presence.

Bucking me as usual to one side;
nothing to grasp or hold to
but rusty hinges; bent nails,
stark on broken gates and posts;
flecks of old paint,
grimy green;
discarded fibro scraps in feathery dust.
Everything used up or incomplete,
lids missing – rubbish really,
broken and done for.
Nothing tidy
on the parched earth.

Hoping for beauty or reward,
shy on the sideline
where the overgrowth
swallows the corrugation,
caressing the cracked and
collapsing tin –
this clamberous furze
of verdigris and magenta –
a resplendent canopy
to enslave the vision,
catching every tipple of sunlight
into its vast parabola,
offering itself unabashed,
ushering me in
to some faint intimation of acceptance.

Matinee

Up the winding stairs,
creaking alarmingly
inside my brain,
second door to the left,
I find that familiar
old play-blanket,
strung,
Punch-and-Judy like,
between the bones of skull,
as we used to hang it –
Gaynor and I –
for puppetry.

I venture in
and sit back
for the show
with some impatience
and more foreboding,
as images dimly advance
on a grey screen,
winding like llama
down marrowed cliffs
to deeper mental slopes.

Yet there is something
behind or beneath
that requires unveiling;
and my hands fail to reach
into the shadow-play –
but clap in confusion
against each other.

The Explorer

Each day at Ashgrove
I would go at lunch-hour
into the screaming jungle;
or from Puddleby-on-the-Marsh
off somewhere to the moon
with Doctor John Dolittle,
who was phased by nothing.

On finishing
the soggy cheese and pickle
my mother had thrown together
in sandwiches that morning,
I might fancy a slice of *Magic Pudding*.
Or climb Blyton's *Faraway Tree* –
'a darker green than usual' –
for one of Moonface's Google Buns
or exploding Toffee Shocks;
and end up in
'The Land of Take-What-You-Want'.

I was the only child
in that little school library,
halfway up the concrete stairs,
as the well-adjusted pupils
outside
wrestled and roared,
forever at home with their rough,
mutual affirmations.

The female librarian
(a spinster no doubt),
looking pityingly at me
day after day
over her big mug of tea
as I reappeared
on cue;
alone and Holmes-like,
scanning the crowded shelves:
Ruby and azure spines.
Carnival titles
on alluring covers.
Crisp lettering
falling like bandits
on creamy pages.

I was immersed
in my grand adventure
inside that sanctuary.
I did not require a companion
or a cricket ball to the face
on the school oval,
safe in my quiet delight.

I needed to escape banality
with Hereford the Wake;
or the Famous Five,
rambling the golden uplands;
or to be off,
hunting with Mowgli
or Tarzan
and all the beasts of the forest,
for a mere sufficiency of survival.

Westerlies (A Rubaiyat)

The winds would turn me inside out,
leapfrogging spirit over doubt.
Due east each August they would come
and leave behind their trail of rout.

Their gift was pure exhilaration.
My heart would swell – a wild sensation.
They swirled inside me like a Dervish
and put all end to relaxation.

The winds would catch me at my back
and spin me down a one-way track
of dancing grass and waving trees
and laughter in the cul-de-sac.

My nose is running as I run
and clouds are racing past the sun.
Red leaves are hurled into the blue
and flying birds tossed in confusion.

Each day at dusk they ceased to blow
and left me in their afterglow.
I'd sit a while to catch my breath
as skies turned ink and indigo.

These winds to me were purely blessing,
keen and free; and yet caressing.
Each year I'd fall to their embrace,
possessed, beset and acquiescing.

Another Sunday

Gibbers; bindi eyes…
patina of dust:
The long afternoon
shimmers before us.

We walk always
into the margins:
Birds with bad throats
shadow us.

Muddled grasshoppers
bump in mid-air.
Bladey-grass yellows
in the sun.

We stretch on flat rocks,
watching the silver creek
slide and glitter,
line-dancing with leaves.

A breeze runs off
with the minutes.
Harvey recalls the sixpence
he found on the tram.

The Vow

Into a tangle of wait-a-whiles,
through the jumble of lantana –
ticks and snakes notwithstanding –
mozzies; the odd stone bruise:

Pffft!

We are fearless –
Lords of this terrain:
us little kids.
So confident amongst
the rough, mint-green leaves,
the harsh, intransigent stems,
the tiny bouquets
of red and yellow blooms
we nonchalantly spin
in our fingers;
the thickets we burrow
expertly through
like wildlife,
born to this place.

In the dusty summer break,
we hollow out
our secret rendezvous
under the tight canopy
of interlaced branches,
squatting together,
we three,
serenely sweating,
swearing fealty
into the drone of the day:
Cutting the pads
of each index finger
gingerly
with a bathroom blade
I stole,
mixing the crimson globules,
vowing on
the blood-trickle
into our palms
never to abandon
this refuge
for adult ways.

This hallowed place
our souls have wedded;
spirits exalted here
in our oval shelter
amid endless days
of rough childhood –
no repercussions
upon our freedom.

Just careless days
of splendour and sunshine;
scabs and scratches,
soft drinks and singing:
and the deeper intoxications
of untamed minds.

Saturday Night

I won't dance.
Don't ask me.
I am far too nervous:
But I will sit
expectantly here
as they wander in.

The Gypsy Taps,
the Pride of Erins,
the unprogressive barn dances
thankfully over
for the evening.

The band at last
opening up.

Sudden energy
flooding the room:
a hubbub now –
a frisson of wildness,
slick with Brylcreem;
flared skirts flying high.

Stand back!
They are coming through
in untamed precision,
like Negroes bursting
from the back of the bus,
possessing the dance floor.

Pumping piano
and brazen saxophones.
Ragged guitars
and this acrimonious drumming…

And
'Good-a-ness gar-acious!'
they are leaping past me…

All lassoed up
in rope petticoats,
spinning out,
twirled high like lariats,
slid across shoulders,
catapulted over hips,
tunnelled between legs
like medicine balls.

Not simply dancers
but gymnasts,
acrobats,
frantically balletic.
The bodgie hairstyles
congealed into immobility
as they jitter-bug and jive.

Unstoppable,
unperturbed;
magisterial
in their power
and bouncy muscularity:
Fag packs in rolled-up sleeves.

The floor trembling
with rock'n'roll fever
beneath their pounding feet,
imprinted forever
under the yellow lights
of the War Veterans' Hall.

Foolish Nightmare

Tangled in my beanstalk dream,
I watch
the tick-tock crayon witch
plunder my quilts
and bunch and gather
a fat, felt creature:
a patchwork beast,
mattress-backed
and pillow-tongued
that she leashes,
cackling,
by only pyjama cords
to my bedhead.

A chequered, woollen wolf
that gollops my novels,
snapping their paperbacks
and cracking hard covers
like pork rind.

Quieter then
and cow-eyed,
it grazes the carpet,
until mooing softly,
it mounts the bed
and spreads at last –
a warm, dry entity –
to recover itself,
and me,
as blanket.

Transition

When we left at last,
stumbling down
our separate roads
to manhood,
would the lank eucalypts,
we wondered,
mark our going
as they had mourned, no doubt,
the passing of the Turrbal,
who once wore these rutted tracks
into the mountain sides
where we had walked?

And the long narrow creek,
trickling and roaring in turn,
whose custodians we became –
would it even register
our sudden absence;
or would other eager boys,
assuming our identities,
step into our ministrations there
with hardly a pause?

The giant tree
standing as a sentinel
where our street –
barely a cart-track
when we arrived –
began,
was brought down
and vanished one day
when I wasn't looking:
Its massive stump
a hillock of ash.
So immense
we three would shelter on occasion
inside its hollowed trunk,
crouching on little haunches,
gazing upward
into the dark, cobwebbed immensity,
as the rain beat down outside.

Were squalling babies
ever birthed at our feet
in here long ago?
We had wondered this.

Was the soccer oval
at Bowman Park –
that vast green circle
at Cobbler's Flat
at the end of our Esplanade –
ever a sacred bora ring,
a mighty hub of dedicated humanity
so close upon the creek and the mountains,
the curling campfires
and the clap-sticks slapping,
echoing interminably out
into the cool, still night?

Here We Go Round the Sun

The Earth:
black-veined,
rough-skinned –
fat drunken gypsy,
spinning about the fire.

Scarred and cragged,
sweating silt of seas.
Juice-jungled hair,
sprouting unkempt,
tendrilled.

Swirling
frayed rags of grief
and gaiety;
lost to the fiddle-chirrups
and tambourine bash…

The raucous hoots
and bronchial bellows –
till the fire,
much later,
softens to ash.

Ooh Ma Soul!

Little Richard Penniman,
once penniless,
never little –
bigger than Texas;
sexier than *Sexus*.

Larger than life:
Punching above his weight,
jumping out of his skin,
standing at his piano
legs akimbo –
flying almost…

Trousers flapping,
head back, bawling,
saxes honking:
Upsetters upsetting.
All zoot suit
and conked hair,
mascara and pomade.

Purely raucous
and raucously pure.
Elemental.
Root cause of
rock'n'roll.

Beverley and I
on the Bardon tram,
loudly lauding Richard
over Elvis,
ignoring jaded adults,
looking askance.
Swaying from leather straps,
looking in each other's eyes:
'Won't you come along with me!'

Harvey and I,
still perplexed
up Outlook Crescent
after twenty spins
of 'Long Tall Sally':
frenzy nevertheless
stirring our DNA
on his front porch;
his mother yelling
through the venetians,
more hysterical
than Richard himself.

Richard on stage,
inciting riot,
ripping up that purple shirt
at Brisbane Stadium.
Richard in white jumpsuit,
jumping through
the hoops of
'Jumping Jack Flash'
at Festival Hall –
ours for another night.

Richard in wheelchair,
no longer jumping,
no longer standing;
yet inside
still jumping, jumping;
still standing,
taller and longer
than 'Long Tall Sally':
Not to be replicated.
Not to be defied:

'I am that I am…
I am all of it…
Shut up! Shut up! Shut up!'

… And the crowds would rise
to the whites of his eyes –
to the whites of his ivories.

Premeditated Siege

Unarmed,
I walk into
an ambush of ferrets –
All around,
weasels and ferrets;
and stoats –
especially stoats:

(They're the ringleaders.)

They sit silently round me
(with their sharp teeth,
in the evening,
in the forest)
watching me starve.

What have I ever done to them?

Brisbane (2017)

This place,
so wretched at times
yet rife with memory:
Summer rushing in again
through the floodgates of spring.
A sky of dark denim today
and white feathers
through my Raybans
as the Black and White cab
and its brown driver
round a Hamilton corner.

And there, suddenly,
this year's first jacaranda,
resplendent,
drenched in the siren colour
of that faded paper rose,
once magenta, now violet,
pinned to Auntie Elsie's
blue dress that evening
in the white, weatherboard house
on the Bardon hill.

Just us there in that bedroom
for a while
and her, shimmering above me
like the Blue Fairy;
a scent of cherry brandy –
a cheap, enveloping perfume –
defining her
as she leans in on my pillow,
brushing hair back
from my forehead,
black tears streaking
her rouged cheeks –
incomprehensible murmurs
and choked sobs.

And me,
wrenched from sleep,
trying to pull together
something consoling
from my modest vocabulary
between those hoarse whispers,
looking down
into the tanned, rutted beauty
of her cleavage,
momentarily,
as she bends forward
uncaring,
and the party rolls on
out in the kitchen.

Coming in to tell me,
her special boy that night,
no doubt,
thinking back on it now,
one last goodbye
from a party
where all went wrong.

Every year
these lavender jacaranda blooms,
their cloying petals
falling, falling…

Always bringing this back.

Contemplation before Annihilation

(Cuban missile crisis, 1962)

Outside, above us all,
the cold, grey rain
is beginning to fall.
But don't look over
at your weatherproofs now.

This time
not proof enough, I fear.

Do you recall streaming nights
of endless rain?
I remember lining
the empty milk bottles
on our doorstep
and the splashings
on my cold, white ankle.

This time
the storm will soak us all.

And do you recall
the symphony of heat
the old sun played
on our liquid pores
as we tanned naked
on the smooth rock slab,
linking little fingers?

Soon the sun
will burst in this room.

I remember
the deep, calm blue
of the sky that day:

Blue and blue and blue
to Infinity

When all the dustmen are dead,
the dust,
the rat-grey dust,
will edge down every seam:
lay shrouds of silence
on broken faces;
grow leaden hills
in open doors and mouths.

If through the heavy air
a wind comes breathing –
a curious whining note –
let us propose
it is only God
blowing his nose:

Fretting
that all his toys are broken.

Lenore (1964)

A coiled swirl of hair,
honey-blonde –
a generous half-hemisphere,
glowing in a torn envelope
for fifty years.

Disturbing it today
with an older finger
than once stroked it,
I could have sworn
it was ashen-grey;
but no –
honey-blonde,
same as it ever was.

You forget.

But there she is
in a photo here,
black and white
on the hood of a flash car
she did not own
in Albert Street
(after handing me her Kent),
posed like a film star
in dark boots and glasses,
on our way to the movies.

Laughing –
almost falling over laughing:
her small, delicate hands
to her chest;
her *Time* magazine
ostentatious,
folded under her arm.

Or:
descending those
rickety
Teneriffe
stairs,
her flaxen hair glimmering
under the yellow,
moth-specked light,
her powder-blue dress
whispering over blue petticoats:
My Blue Angel for tonight,
coming towards me,
head cocked slightly,
quizzical grin
at this gobsmacked Jiminy Cricket
gazing up, below her.

'Len,' I said.
'Len' was all that I said.

Or:
dancing down
the cool asphalt,
swirling along
ghostly suburban streets
together at 3 a.m.
after another crazy party
to some show tune
from *My Fair Lady*
or *Carousel*.

Both in lockstep,
not a foot wrong:

*'So Mister,
Mister DJ,
Keep those records playing.*

*… And me and my baby,
We're out here on the floor.'*

New Find

Gravediggers
struck oil
in the graveyard.
Gravely,
probes were lowered
and cemetery shares soared.

Black geysers
shot coffins aloft,
spattering mourners
(already funereal).
Corpses, like sponges,
sucked in the spill:

Monuments besmirched!
Urns polluted!
Fresh headstones reading,
'Not Dead – Only Seeping.'

Petroleum trucks,
in endless cortège,
wound reverentially
through the gates.

Undertakers
undertook a solemn protest:

The drilling, they said,
was killing their business.

Dawn Service

Mascara ran down her cheek
as the waves,
indistinct in the pre-dawn light,
caressed the cold sand.

Lazy filigrees of foam
almost at our naked feet
as we huddled together
on that inadequate hotel towel,
waiting for the sun.

I had gone down with her,
anticipating some
Burt Lancaster moment
at the crashing surf's edge:
only twenty after all
with no mastery of empathy
over lust…

And even as she quietly wept,
my eyes were on
her shapely legs –
her ample skirt
pulled back carelessly –
or, what I had dearly hoped,
provocatively,
across her pale, open thighs.

Only our upper arms touched
as we settled together
on that chill shore
and she spoke of her mad,
drunken father
and the shame – as it then was –
of an illegal abortion:
and the general futility
in that moment
of everything else.

What did I reply?

I do not remember a word,
though, no doubt, words were said…

Only a sense of her fragile body,
like some exhausted seabird
that had wheeled in
from a distant place
across that vast ocean
and landed, inexplicably, there beside me.

Vietnam Days

(After Gregory Corso)

I am so far from NAPALM…

So far from 'Commie-get-your-gun:
Here come
The Berets' posse!'
It's hard to see…

It's a disarming,
unalarming
(doubtlessly charming)
sort of word:

'NAPALM'…

Just listen –
(with careful enunciation…)

'*Neigh*-PALM'…

glossy, buckskin leaves –
horses drinking round
some cool oasis…

Or '*Nah*-PALM'…

almost,
(though not quite):
Jesus of *Nah*-zareth;
Palm Sunday
on holy, lowly mule.

But
it's not like that really…

NAPALM:

Graduating straight
from Harvard
to you –
(well, not really *you* –
unless of course
under friendly fire –
and that HAS happened) –
but to THEM,
always to THEM…

And,
in fact,
it's quite a horror-show
from the pictures.

BAM! BAM! BAM!

Children who don't
any more
look like children –
who look more like
I Was a Teenage Bonfire –
X-rated viewing.
Not for general exhibition…

I bet the president
wouldn't let his daughter
marry one
even slightly singed.

But then again,
How do we know
they are real –
and not some
'Commie-Toffee-Meltee-Dummies'?

Has anyone seen one MOVE?

(*'NAPALM! NAPALM!*
It's icky sticky goo.
Napalm! Napalm!
It always sticks to THEM!')

All the Way (1966)

LBJ is late tonight,
very late…

We sit
on the Queen Street pavement
like Vladimir and Estragon
this warm evening,
our backs against granite.

And so we patiently wait,
reading of Bertrand Russell,
de Beauvoir and Satre,
and their approaching
War Crimes Tribunal
to try this man
and others like him
in absentia –
this man
now approaching us –
for abomination in Vietnam.

So they will sit
in judgment of the napalm scars,
covering the small body
of DoVan Ngoc –
a nine-year-old –
and every machination
of this 'industrial colossus'
attacking 'a small peasant nation'.

Three million pounds
of bombs
raining daily down:
'chemicals and gas,
napalm, phosphorus…
fragmentation weapons
and bacteriological devices'
pouring onto North Vietnam
as we wait.

So, next month,
in Stockholm
and Roskilde,
Scandinavia –
as a 'moral authority'
without state power –
they will sit in judgment
of this man,
as we sit in like judgement
in Brisbane, Queensland,
tonight
as he approaches us.

Lyndon Baines Johnson
on the first presidential tour.

Yet he has been here before:
Brisbane, Rockhampton,
Mackay. Townsville,
Charters Towers, Winton…
He has seen them all
some two decades ago,
confronting a more
legitimate foe.
He even got a Silver Star
for dropping bombs
on 'native buildings'
at Salamaua,
eighty miles shy of target.

But where is he tonight?
The spectator lines
are surprisingly thin
along our main thoroughfare;
as, in southern cities,
war-mad crowds,
larger than Beatlemania,
have mobbed
his 'bottle-top'
Lincoln Limousine,
showering confetti
and ticker tape
down on him
in supine replication
of New York.

While others –
a smaller crew
with their caustic signs:
'Welcome Lady Bird
and Butcher Bird',
have lain down
before his cavalcade,
bedecking it
with red and green paint,
incurring public wrath
in a nation
fattened on lies,
marching in lockstep
with him through Vietnam.

This is only Brisbane.
But we must do something tonight.

Saturday evening draws on;
and now crowds
are pouring from the cinemas,
filling the sidewalk.

So, at last
they can bring him up
to a respectable display of fuss,
stopping a while down there
at MacArthur's corner
(where Diggers
trounced Yanks in '42)
before sailing majestically on
through the cheers
towards us.

So few here
opposing all this;
but we run,
Kay and I,
directly at his
shiny black beetle,
creeping past the Regent.
And for an instant
I seem to lay my palm
on the window,
catching his face,
beaming, safe inside.

But like gnats,
we are swatted away
by his grim agents,
jogging alongside,
and knocked to the street.

So that is it then?
Is this all we can do?

'Run!' Kay yells,
pulling me from the road
as the car disappears.
So we run,
fast on young legs
towards Lennon's
by a back route,
as his entourage
turns into George Street.

And we are running
through the Old Town Hall Arcade,
across Adelaide Street,
past Clark Rubber,
along an unnamed alley,
running, running,
racing the president
to his hotel suite.

We arrive
behind a clamouring crowd,
tight packed
at the entrance,
as Johnson alights
to a red carpet.
And, without halting,
Kay propels us forward,
burrowing somehow through
a packed and yelling mass,
parting eerily before
her onrush,
dragging me behind.

And always on towards Johnson…

Two trajectories
intersecting now
at right angles
in Lennon's doorway.
He is so tall,
so perpendicular,
as he strides forward
through the hubbub,
nearly home…

But she rears up,
almost into his face,
and with all inside her,
howls one word,
half-snarl, half-scream,
so emphatic and close
the spittle hits his cheek:
'MURDERER!'

Then, instantaneously,
she faints
straight down,
like some detonated building,
at his feet.

(Speaking truth to power
this will come to be known.)

In the instant
of that word –
that enraged yawp –
and, as she vanishes away
before me,
I see him blanch.
I catch his distinct recoil,
this president:
his eye darting
in momentary alarm.
His face pulling away
from that roaring voice
as if his time has come.

Just us –
and especially her –
and the most powerful man
in the world
in Brisbane tonight;

and no one else here
in that second, to record it:
A protest more potent
than paint thrown;
more intimate
than lying in the road
before a motorcade.
Stepping for that instant
right through his defences
into his private sphere –
his assured and sanitised world,
confronting the heart
of deceit and doubt…

A tiny, glancing blow
for North Vietnam –
and DoVan Gnoc…

Yet the delirious crowd
hardly notice the attack,
paying us little heed
in their excitement,
as they pass her limp body,
as though rejoicing,
hand over hand
like some casualty
from a mosh pit,
propping her down
on the cool cement
against a concrete
flowerpot,
where, alone now,
I bring her round
at last.

So I tell it all here again,
just as it happened –
or as best I can recall
from fifty years ago –
to let you know
that here in Brisbane
we did well that night.
We did our best.

Memory

Slides away.
Sheds its skin.
Appears in dreams.
Breaks into shards.

Is re-formed.
Repeats itself.
Is isolated hours
marooned in time.

Is myself small.
Is me running,
then fighting.
Then wrapped in another.

Is the smell
of a book.
Is a cinema seat,
swathed in darkness.

Is laughing
over nothing.
Is sobbing
into a mirror.

Is the grip of fear
on a hostile road.
Is being
engulfed by love.

Is dancing wildly
for hours.
Is singing softly
to myself.

Is farewelling
a lover.
Is addressing
a surly crowd.

Is forgetting
everything
on every side
of the memory.

Is a moment
reborn, full of itself.
Is gradually
fading to white.

Epiphany

(On first hearing The Band)

In those days
things only got better.
We were headed for
The Golden Age.

And there we were
back then…
A war on –
that hideous war.
Assassinations:
John, Bobby and Martin;
Patrice, Malcolm and Che.

And everywhere,
that racist mosaic –
a marbled monument to hate.
Women trapped in aspic,
second-class.
Gays casually molested,
skilled in camouflage.
Climate and environment
imperceptibly degrading…

But
we
had
it
covered.

Nothing impossible
in that gilded time,
that age of impossibility,
as our righteous music,
bore us forward,
caressing us;
our delights made
commonplace:
blessing us daily,
endorsing our worth
beyond doubt.
Whole world erupting
through booming speakers,
off shiny vinyl.

Stories abounding…

Twisting with Chubby onstage.
Dylan's corrosive drawl,
miles away from Motown,
bewildering in its rawness –
that unfamiliar joint
alight in my fingers.
Or first hearing Otis
one grey afternoon,
the rain teeming down,
in Jill's small flat
by the river.

Howlin' Wolf
in black and white,
confounding the Stones
on *Shindig*!
And the Beatles,
up on that roof,
singing their last and best
into the winds of change,
wild hair whipping about,
each now uncloned
from the rest...

But now I am climbing
the rickety back stairs
of a weatherboard house
set high on wooden stumps...

Inside,
sprawled on the floor
at a low table,
long hair cascading
over square granny glasses,
an angular, intense woman,
dressed flowingly
(as was the style),
industriously rolling joints.

She looks up,
smiling slightly
as we enter –
Rosie and I.

Beams of gold light,
arching through
a bead-glass curtain,
door-length,
throw chromatic flashes
across pine-wood walls:
ruby, turquoise, aquamarine,
amber.

Offstage,
an alchemy
of serpentine voices,
drifting in
from the next room,
crisp and distinct,
projecting darting shadows
from some weird, lost time,
unknown to us.

So…
consider the crystalline moment:

Lyn, in full, free-fall mode,
her long legs splayed
on the shining floor:

'Big Pink,' she explains.

The late afternoon sun
scattering into every
sparkling array,
stippling the room where we stand,
Rosie and I
(already stoned by it –
though nothing yet lit).

And this spectral music,
wondrous and worn,
swirling round us
like fragrant smoke
in that ordinary room.
Our souls climbing
onto the broad backs
of those half-broken voices,
hard-polished
like cracked leather,
or dusty antiques
of burnished wood,
splintered with age,
sequestered away
in long-forgotten cabins.

Civilisation

A lion roars
in a jungle clearing
and tears a hind leg
off a yearling.

Around their fire
some cannibals squat,
lifting limbs
from their cooking pot.

And we sit down
to our veal again
and pity those bulls
in those bullfights in Spain.

Lost Nights

When we would gather
those Friday evenings,
so primed for pleasure
and bring in albums and laughter,
with bottles opening
and acrid fragrance
throughout the rooms…

When there was this
constant procession
of everyone
through the green front door:
The town's misfits arriving,
gay and transient and transgender,
black and radical,
hippie and high,
lesbian, straight and confused,
trooping in,
shedding camouflage,
becoming themselves
for another short while –
another endless night…

As we sat together in groups,
talking in low tones
around the jade chesterfields,
increasingly inchoate,
yet somehow always witty,
rolling against each other
in variations of bliss;

or dancing in clumps
on the trembling floor,
conscientiously
impressing our youth
into the grain
of that timber.

And for every
forgotten conversation;
every beat of that music
from big pine speakers,
booming and fading away…
each puff and mouthful,
each touch and impression
somehow congealed
into lavish recollection
of satin and emerald,
lace, silk or denim,
tassels and bangles,
jasmine and carmine,
powder and lip gloss,
bulges and muscle,
confessions; some kisses…

And drunken, drugged
declarations of allegiance
to each other
and to all that has since gone
from everywhere now
but in the grain of that wood
beneath the old mustard carpet;
and the little
attic storerooms
we have each hidden away –
those who are left –
inside us.

1788 and All That

Seventeen-seventy.
Seventeen-eighty-eight:
Nicely rounded figures,
slotted snugly into the brain,
rolling easily off the tongue.

Lodged like implants:
Cook and Phillip hard-wired,
summoned on command
(One with knife in throat;
the other with spear in chest,
but no matter).

'Discovery'/'Settlement' –
no need for contemplation.
Then moving briskly forward.
('Mind the blood there!')
No intervening impediments,
save for the annual stopover
at some Turkish beach,
dodging whining bullets.

History:
a dance floor
where the present pirouettes
round the past:

Lest we remember.
Lest we forget.

I do remember
that enrolment crisis
in History…

The American
from Japanese Studies –
his cunning plan:
'If forced to teach
Australian History,
I will stand at the podium.
I will open the textbook.
Call out:
"Captain Cook discovered Australia!"
Slam shut the book.
March out.'

Still a closed book to most…

In that sanctum,
they agreed confidently,
'Race was unimportant here.'
Sometimes adding,
'No violent frontier!'

I was there in that staffroom.
I heard these things:
'Those raking up past misdeeds
are hair-shirt delinquents.'
That was my milieu,
my working life,
planted in bitter topsoil
for forty-odd years.
Little changing in a hurry…

Anyway

Outside, meanwhile,
the hearty laughter,
showing white teeth,
wriggling fitfully
on the hook of History,
confident of escape.

No sanctuary for grim tidings
or self-doubt.

All inured against pain
not theirs:
'It is hard to quarrel
with those who only wish
to be innocently happy'

Truth holding little purchase
in a land of raging certainties
where the living
smile and block
the shouts of the dead.

In a country
where 1788 never ends.

Brisbane (1861)

Along the new roads,
mere cart-tracks
on ancient pathways,
they stumble and fall,
their bullock-hearts bursting,
dying on their knees
amid the cicada drone.

Unharnessed
from a team
of twenty, perhaps thirty,
and rolled aside.

Native dogs and carrion crows
squabble around each carcass,
picking it clean.
Giant skeletons,
gleaming in sunlight,
dubbed in bleak sarcasm
'Colonial Milestones'.

Ruddy and bearded men
in red and blue serge
register nothing
but wool and fat wethers;
beef or fast horses.

They curse and bellow
as drays,
top-heavy with bales,
bog in Queen Street mud.

Bullock teams everywhere,
straining forward.
The bullwhips
cut through hide
and the blood spurts.

They land with relief
from the rat-raddled ships,
sailing through estuarine waters,
sluggish with mangroves,
resembling Louisiana bayous.

The serpentine river,
broad as the Thames
at Westminster,
winds past country
duplicating Blackheath:
picturesque –
gardens of Indian corn
and cotton;
others falling back to grass.

Dolphin and shark
up the river,
dugong and turtle,
swooping birds,
voices cracked by heat.
Skies blue as today.

Yet the town dismays.
Thoroughfares leading nowhere,
disfigured by stumps;
new landscapes of wasteland.
Streets of ruts and ravines.
Slopes steep, without drainage.
Sewage and miasma,
rank with foul smells.

Greasy mutton chops;
adulterated spirits.
Men paid in rum –
water 'like liquid manure'.
Slum-dwelling abounding;
tumbledown shanties,
more artless
than the dwellings they displace…

Mere skeleton frames
without doors or windows,
cobbled together
from biscuit boxes
and wine casks,
roofed with zinc and iron;
tinder for conflagration
in grim lanes
and back streets:
An entire 'sanitary mistake',
hostage to fire and flood.

People listless
as their river,
dodging sunstroke,
mosquito-bitten,
torpid with the plainest living.

Everything makeshift,
half-formed and still.

Nothing normal.

Newcomers warned:
'Be careful whom you know.'
A 'bad element' preponderating –
wild-looking strangers
in from the backblocks
and raw Irish.

Rowdies roaring;
open whoring.
Men fight with
stock-whips in the street.
Women brawl with broomsticks.
Aborigines dance for a sixpence.

The night peppered with gunshot
as possums tumble from trees.
And overhead
the great black clouds,
the legions of flying fox,
headed for the islands of the Bay,
pass silently on.

War Correspondent

'I will let them know there is a Hill on the field.' – T.H. Hill, Cairo to Mother, North Sydney, 12 August 1915

Private Tommy Hill,
armed and ready for the kill,
sails off to far Gallipoli,
writing to his mother,
and not for any other,
to read out to an eager family:

'Dears,
Do not worry over Tom…
I will get through alright…'

On an ANZAC troopship
and soon about to land,
he writes back home to Neutral Bay
in a clearly shaky hand,

'Don't be frightened.
I will be alright…
From your loving son
off to do his duty,
Tom.'

Then, later in the trenches,
he is thinking of Mum's dinners
and feeling '*safe as churches*' now,
hopes his dad is picking winners.
He'll be home '*without a scratch*' eventually:

*'Just dying for the good
old evenings that we had.
Don't feel down
because I'm away.
I'll be OK
and arrive back safe and sound –
Then what a dinner
we'll all have, eh?'*

Insisting he will see no harm,
takes shrapnel in the hip and arm.
Bears it quietly '*like a Briton*'
and, walking with a stick,
tells all his mates, '*Don't worry.
It's only just a nick.*'

'*Father, old boy,
we're a good double now.
Mine's the same side as yours.
When you receive this
it will be Christmas Day
or close handy.
I wish I was sharing in the dinner…*'

Corporal Tom Hill,
now mentioned in despatches,
evacuates Gallipoli
among the final batches.
Anxious for a war to win,
sailing off to France,
hopes to '*drive the bayonet in*'
when given half a chance:

'How is the garden?
I hope the chokos are on
when I get back…
I would like to be home
for a feed of chokos…
We can have a few bottles
and enjoy them, eh?'

At Pozières, Sergeant Tom Hill,
shell fragments lodged within his thigh,
is destined for another spill,
yet crosses for another try:
He shows no mercy – super keen –
a primed and ready war machine:

'It's good sport, Father,
when the bayonet goes in…
But, for heaven's sake,
keep John and Arthur back.
I have got their share of Germans –
and no more fronts
like the Somme for sure.'

But the war grinds on
and without fail,
they get his medal in the mail.
And Tom, still sure he'll see it through,
now finds himself at Passchendaele:

'I think it will end
by next winter;
but if it takes ten years,
we will lick 'em…'

Hard as a rock and fourteen stone,
the bullets slice him to the bone.
They pull him from the sucking mud.
Later he dies from loss of blood.

Back home that day, the weather's fine.
The chokos ripen on the vine.

The quotations used in this poem are taken from letters written by Thomas Hill to his parents in North Sydney. They can be found in *Letters written on Active Service. European War 1914–18* (AL) Mitchell Library, Sydney.

Missing in Action (1918)

Nothing of him
ever returned:
Not a skerrick.
Not even the pumping aorta
the shrapnel severed.

(Of course, there had been
no guaranteed return ticket
when signing up.)

He had never really wanted
to come home
with missing limbs
or no eyes
or a brain gone permanently AWOL
in any case.

And the chances
of getting back exactly
as he'd left –
so spruce and able
and full of mustard –
were now somewhat remote.

So, as he ran forward
on strong legs
into the bullet spray
as ordered,
he had already
sent his mind off elsewhere,
eyes closed.
And whispering calmly
as he ran,
suddenly on tiptoes,
the soothing mantra:
'The goose that laid
the golden egg…'

As he had sung it
over and over
in that high-pitched,
sing-song voice of his
on those shining afternoons
when his mother was
still the goose
on their wild, raucous
'goose chases'
round the backyard;
and the anaemic sun
up there
the blazing golden egg.

Deliverance

'Had the Japs invaded,'
she quietly intones,
bending over the
hot cup of tea,
'our idea was
to quit Mossman
quick smart –
go bush, you know.
Live in the wilds
like Abos…
My husband's best plan
was to follow
this bridle track –
an old Aboriginal trail –
into the interior.
"They'd never find us,"
he said.'

A blowfly
butts at the screen.
She blows and sips.

An old Aboriginal trail
to escape the Japs
as successfully
as the irony of it all
continues to escape her.

Frontier (1868)

The Sniders yet to be ordered
with their half-million shells,
big as elephant cartridges,
from the War Office…

So the Terry's breech-loaders,
made in Birmingham,
already seeing good service
in New Zealand,
will have to do.

A dry midwinter's day
up here in the Gulf.

Wentworth D'Arcy Uhr
and his trooper band
on patrol,
chasing down Waanji-Garawa
who have 'cut steaks
from the rumps'
of several horses.

We cannot have this
out here in the Gulf.

So 'upwards of thirty'
dispatched at first
by Minie bullets
from the Terrys'
for such brash indiscretion.

In retaliation, then,
(as is the custom here),
one of Little and Hetzer's men,
Cameron,
is speared
out on the Norman.

So mobs are rounded up
for execution.
Clearly, Uhr means business:
Fourteen falling
in the first assault;
then a further nine
as the rifles bark and snap.
And, finally, another eight –
all snuffed out in a batch.

One warrior,
against all odds
in an urgency to live,
refuses to fall.
'Eighteen or twenty bullets',
the Burketown correspondent
breathlessly calculates,
are received,
striking him from all sides
as stumbling, balletic,
torn to a pulp,
he will not submit
to the logic
of leaden ordnance.

Such big bullets too:
each a .537 calibre.

So a native policeman
steps judiciously in,
wielding his Terry's stock,
and brings an end
to the stubborn defiance
by smashing in his skull.

All in the township
and out on the stations
are delighted
at the gory calculus:
Upwards of sixty 'myalls'
for one white man
and some lost horses –
a sterling credit balance
for the account sheet
(a balance the frontier
will blandly repeat).

So, volubly,
they crowd Mr Uhr
at this news of overkill
with toasts of gratitude
for the energy applied
to such 'wholesale slaughter'.

Little noticing, as they rejoice,
a monstrous illness, closing
around them,
eventually
killing upwards of sixty –
and, incidentally,
their town as well.

Imagination

Sailing on a turquoise sea
with everyone
I'd like to be.

Standing on an ice-strewn shore,
waiting for
the summer thaw.

Climbing up a sheer rock wall,
with not a care
that I might fall.

Running from a wild wolf pack,
anticipating
some attack.

Wandering through a glistening cave,
with no necessity
to be brave.

Sitting in a field of rye,
with little children
running by.

Rolling down a grassy slope,
so elated;
high on dope.

Lying in another's bed,
amazed at all
that I just said.

Sheltering from torrential rain,
with a steaming bowl
of shrimp chow mein.

Stranded on a jungle isle,
with a very
patient necrophile.

Watching kestrel in their flight
turn to fireflies
at twilight.

Intercourse

The swung breast:
A sac of white honey
teases a needy mouth –
Lips enclosing finally
a turgid nipple,
eager to express itself
in imaginary,
propulsive jets
of sweetness.

We settle,
bodies aslant,
head to breast
of comparative size,
locked in
intimate communion.
Your fingers
at first
parting my moist lips;
and then slow suckling
beginning,
satisfying both
in illusions
of endless transfer.

The tongue,
a hot under-groove
for the pretend spendings.
The teeth,
so eager
to leave a sharp, urgent mark.
Your thighs opening then,
expelling the clitoral horn,
rising through wetness,
eager to take
its rigid stand
inside the eye of
a thick penile head…

You whisper urgently
of the sweet pre-come,
ejecting so easily
into your hand
as you explore
the loose, fleshy hood.
Your hot tongue
going deep in my ear –
and I am almost undone…

So the old cock,
reaching a jerking
height of achievement
for today,
shoots back
its pale, pearly tribute
over dark hairs
and soft, white belly:
striations of
snail-silver,
delivered staccato
from navel to vulva;
a mixed earth odour
of spunk and rut,

infusing
lushly then
the dark burrows of sleep.

The Visit

I am drawn
to the blackness
of your hair,
an acute sheen –
thick and glossy like Elvis,
shiny today like anthracite.
Dusty gold skin –
at close quarters,
a scent of musk and spice.

Shadowed by images
of your broken past,
I swim into
the blackness of your eyes.
I set sail there
in full confidence:
A landlubber,
guiding his fragile vessel,
who will be unalarmed
should he slip overboard.

I know your small hand
will reach out,
guiding me back to the boat;
or, tumbling laughing
into the waves with me.

We sink into salty blueness,
Van Morrison bringing
your lips to mine.

Finally
teeth ripping surprisingly
at my mouth,
spasming under my hands,
growling feebly
and falling
into the deep ocean's slumber.

Uncatalogued Nightmare

'Reach for me!'
the blood slides over
a sheet of smooth foil,
silver-white and frosted.

Searing, silent grief,
skirting its old wound,
probes a dull blade
of indifference.

Ashes rain silently down
on abject tenements.

The blood freezes:
a bright sheen of vermilion.
The joints compass outward
and break free…

The trunk tumbles,
spouting down stone steps,
bouncing into the spider arms
of the creature reaching for me.

Rain Dance

Waking into thunder,
eyes still closed,
I saw again
her and the rain
as she was leaving me,
turning back momentarily
through a slate-grey drizzle,
her long hair bedraggled;
her amiable face
in that moment askew:
a rictus of grief or guilt.

The swish of traffic
on the rainswept street;
the pat-pattering on the leaves –
everything now punctuated
by this downpour,
spattering my face.

Everything else absorbed
into that saturation.
Something she seemed to say –
her last words –
lost in the deluge.
Then her receding back,
a monochrome,
hurrying into the gloom,
vanishing,
as I stand there,
hostage to the indelible tableau…

Not the blackguard this time,
holding comically
onto my briefcase
as if to keep upright.
Time bending around me,
not registering much else
or seeking shelter.
Just standing,
not dancing, in the rain.

Separate Tables

(for M)

Was it the table you climbed onto
for money;
or fell against
as the knife slashed
your small body?

Or where you sat,
keeping track
in your accounts
of the couplings,
as doors opened and closed?

Or bent over
and wept
when a heavy hand
and harder revelations
slammed into your face?

Or was it the kitchen table
where books of tables
lay open for study;
and the meals served on it
over and over?

And big smiles
on two small faces,
looking up,
mined laughter at last
from your heart's depth?

And kept looking at you
and into you
around that table,
until the hardest part
of everything dissolved again
into the brighter gambles of possibility…

Mother

Maisie 'was dead
to begin with.
There was no doubt
whatever
about that…'

Dead but I won't lie down,
she'd declare,
bending over the bosh
or coming in
from the line…
but now she was both:
Both down and dead –
Gone-a-widdy-coop…

Or perhaps…
Gone where the gooz-gogs go –
Off with those gypsies
in their rainbow caravan;
or marching in the Mardi Gras
to Mantovani strings.

Elbowing me impatiently
out of the way
of some kitchen task:
Let the dog see the rabbit!
Or, face contorted in disgust:
Ach-a-vee-bo-bydo –
as she negotiated
one more dirty nappy.
Everything was
shit-colour drab
in bucolic Bardon –
from the eucalypts
to our latest wear…
And yet, to my sister,
all gussied up for some party:
*You look like
a streetcar named desire…*

(*You had to laugh…
The more you cry,
The less you pee…*)

Bardon was where
*a spaceship
could land
and no one would know…*

And, as memory faltered,
it all became
What-i-coll…

you had to know…

Old age does not come alone,
she would intone,
as everything subsided
except a volcanic temper,
erupting predictably
in its lava flow
over the house…

I am going to scrag-maul you!
– A wild, vengeant spirit
pursuing me down the passage;
a fiery particle,
hurling its puny weight
against my bedroom door,
bending the lock.

When she died at ninety-one
and her body lay,
stiff and stiffening,
I went gingerly in
one last time to say something –
maybe goodbye.

Her jaw was clenched.
(*Get that jib off your puss!*)
Pale lips clamped together.
(*You have got a mouth on you!*)
Her body tensed for take-off.
A face frozen
in a grimace of rage,
like a White Walker
who could no longer walk.

I tried some mollifying words,
standing there, awkward,
heart pounding…
(*You Slunge!*);
speaking diplomatically
to a corpse
as though posterity were listening in.

Yet keeping my distance
nevertheless
from that hospital bed,
as if the eyes would suddenly open,
hands grab for my shirt
and a voice would promise:
Now I'll have your guts for garters!

Passing Through

One went, as through a trapdoor,
hanging by electric cord.
Several fell slowly apart inside.
Another, walking to the beach,
fell in the street…

Falling away, one by one…

One crushed beneath a truck
on a lonely mountain side.
Two simply over-dosing.
One eviscerated
by medical misadventures.
One leaving without warning
easily, in his sleep.
Another leaving a note
beneath some coins:
'For the Vultures'
before he drowned:
His best friend choosing
a car's back seat
with engine running.

So many of them.

Emphysema took one.
Heartbreak, her partner,
soon after.
Another left,
heart-stoppingly,
in a stationary car,
buckled in her seat.
Dementia claimed one:
Her brother,
…once a best friend,
plagued by debt,
exiting in the kitchen.

So much sadness…

And, in this life,
precious pieces chipped away
one by one –
once part of me:
Dark little holes.
Wind blowing in
through smashed windows.

More than a dozen now –
maybe a score.

That chill breeze
I try daily to ignore
eating to the bone,
blowing at the cliff's edge.

Along it
the next generation stand, waiting.
The New Front Line
clutching their Tickets to Ride.

My parents both leaving
in the night…
uncles and aunts
who grew me up
departing somewhere
beyond my knowing:
One alone
on the lounge room floor,
the cricket on.
One in her chair,
head back,
cold cup in hand,
one bite from her biscuit…

Varieties innumerable…

And maybe all picnicking
together right now,
high on a hill somewhere
in some green paddock
with lots of shade.

I hope so.

Don't get me started on the dogs.

Gifts

Sometimes
I almost hear
a purr behind your smile.
It spreads lavishly
over your face,
creasing to receive it;
sometimes even ripening
into a laugh
that throws back your head
and inhabits you.

I want to take it
in my hands
and press it to my chest.

I look into your eyes
more than to any other part
of you –
more than any other part…

No. Rather they look into me,
widening as if
exploring Aladdin's cave.
They mine precious jewels in me
I thought I had lost.

I want to take them all
in my hands
and give them to you.

But it is your voice
that most impels:
Gently clipped African inflections,
soft, careful, unexpected
in what they say:
flowing through me like a salve
as I recover myself;
reminding me of lost things
I have yet to tell
but always wanting to say;
silencing me to listen.

I hold our voices
cupped in my hands
where they splash together
like joyous, golden fish.

Chinese High Noon

I chat with Didi in Kaifeng,
watching, as we talk,
a naked beggar
dancing.

A curious crowd gathers.
His begging bowl fills.
The day is cold:
Ten degrees only
in Communist China.

He is naked.
He is not deranged.
'He dances that way,' says Didi,
'to attract the eyes.'

He is not disabled.
'So why,' Didi asks:
'does he do this?
Is he too lazy
to work with his hands?'

She has seen this before
outside her café.
Others she has seen there
have danced naked too.

Many beggars once.
Now only a few…
'He must dance naked
for the money to come,'
she tells me:

'Dancing clothed
has no novelty
or charm
in Communist China now.'

So he dances naked
on the street to survive.
Police now arrive
to drag him away.

Could this be Mao's Last Dancer?

Requiem

It had not always been this way:

Hands, gnarled, twisted, old
had once bruised men, clasped iron,
pleased women.

Eyes, sunken, watering, squint
had shone in sunlight –
shone sombre, sparkling.

She had said,
'Your eyes have a crisp, clear blueness.
They cut through me, my darling.'

She who now is dead,
one evening, that year,
long ago.

And he had walked,
not bent, rheumatic, crippled
but with a thud of thigh, calf and sinew.

And laughter was pealing and rich
that now rattled, not often,
in a dry, leathered throat.

It was just in mind
that youth now ranged,
unbridled as always – wild and free,

while he shuffled and mumbled
through the shopping mall.

'Dream On'

I love your feet.
I love your nose.
I love the gaps
between your toes.
I love your voice:
your distant pose.
I love your second-handed clothes.

You don't love me:
that heaven knows!
I propositioned:
Your face froze…
But that is just the way it goes:
I'm older now –
and boy, it shows.
My skin is slack
while your skin glows.

My chances shrink.
Your prospect grows.
Your future opens.
My days close.
Inside my head,
my youth still flows;
I yearn for 'Yes!'
yet field the blows –
the kindly stalling
of your 'Noes'.

I sit surrounded
by my crows
and see your body
in its throes.
That image haunts
without repose…
(I know I'm bad!
I knows! I knows!)
I sit and sip
my D-Ribose,
then climb the stairs
and start to doze.

That's what's called Ageing
I suppose…

Last Night

I was captive
inside vast chambers
of the enormous dream,
pacing long corridors
of chipped laminate:
Their slippery, polished floors
sloping away
into deep, hanging stairwells.

I had for safety
to keep to a grey,
concrete corridor,
gripping the winding,
iron balustrade
to hold my balance.

In one room
I began stroking
a wary, amber beaver
(or was it some edgy raccoon?)
He caught my hand
beneath his ample chin,
his dark eye
daring me to complain.
I could not budge it
and regretted my bravado…

Outside,
through a grimy window,
a profusion of blooms:
bougainvillea, jasmine, jacaranda –
tapestries of colour,
shimmering in sharp sunlight
I could not reach.

And inside,
an urgency
to regain my old workplace,
calling for a taxi
that never arrived;
my papers dripping
with some dark treacle,
seeping inside my briefcase;
hopelessly incapable now
of delivering
the lecture on Trotsky
I had agreed upon.

Haiku

Broken houses tilt,
fat frogs peering between stumps.
Primrose gleams through cracks.

The moon slides away.
The old dog stretches and yawns.
Icicles forming.

Dancing on my screen:
Hair floats, whirling black and sleek,
legs striding to me.

Gentle rain, like mist.
The water dragon enters.
The crow's feathers shine.

Days begin to glow.
Parrots return for berries.
Water inviting.

Possum on the roof.
She slips into the warm pool,
one toenail still red.

Dilemma

From a crumbling house,
laced with flowering vines,
I behold glorious nature.
The sun illumines the glittering leaves.
Clouds float like torn gauze.
Lizards galloping past me,
the length of my foot.
Crows, the sheen of shiny coal,
diving for mango scraps.
Squabbling parrots,
too colourful to be real
in their effortless arrogance.

I am surrounded by life:
the cat angling again for food;
the water-dragon and goanna
alternating at his bowl
as he watches.
The ants, defying the pest controller,
commandeering the sink once more.
The odd butterfly,
blue as Paul Newman's eyes,
balletic in mid-air.
Possums climbing noisily
inside walls,
bumping and scraping at night,
stampeding on the tin roof
as a lone mosquito
sucks on my thumb.

I protect them all
as best I can
from the developers –
the easy desperadoes,
who, like Mongols,
will destroy this little world
when I am gone.
The scrub turkey will return
to concrete and brick.
Huge majestic trees,
without a struggle,
will crash groaning to earth.
All returning to sterility:
Possums, lizards, parrots and crows
will flee or perish.
Insects ground to dust…

How could anyone desert them
on this tiny sliver of the planet
where I hold the trust of dominion?

September 2001

(For Ren)

God help me –
not much of a navigator
apparently:
the map I sent
a bum steer,
sending you careering off
down Boggo Road
and into the bowels
of Brisbane.

But eventually,
against all odds,
you found the tree
and there you were.

On a crisp and glorious day:
and the majestic tree,
a perfect parabola,
shining emerald
in the sunlight
on a little rise,
green all about.

And you sitting there
on your picnic blanket,
legs patiently folded
under you
in the shade beneath it
as I climbed from the taxi
with my bulging picnic basket
and came forward.

A meeting drenched
in auspicious beginnings
(and occasional magic)
though you could not eat the food;
and our talk tumbled about
like pups on a blanket;
and the eventual kiss,
so easy and proficient
as if rehearsed many times
to become pitch perfect
and smoothly choreographed.

Time was not of the essence
but firmly on our side that day
in the rounded shadow;
the hours chimed only
by bird cries
and the incessant insect hum.
Dappled sunlight
falling through jade leaves
onto your face.

There were black and white
feathers hanging
in your old car
as I guided us
unerringly home.

Life (2017)

These days
I barely seem to look up,
let alone ahead,
curling mostly inside
this cocoon of pain:
All mine –
yet each day different,
inexplicable
with no forward progress,
evading control.

Some bright mornings
beginning well enough
then evaporating.
Some doomed from waking.
Is this illness or ageing,
or some cruel collaboration
of both?

Fond friends vanish.
Surrounded by suburban hills,
so steep now to climb,
I rarely venture out.
Eyes blur and head pulses.
Nerves and muscles
jangle and throb.

Remembering today
for some reason
August 1964 –
a half-century past –
Lenore on my arm
as we crested that hill
in Victoria Park
(once York's Hollow),
the Annual Show up ahead.

Perhaps a dozen of us
in a sweeping line,
impromptu,
Cinemascope style –
us two in the middle,
all linking arms
singing on cue
(at my instigation),
'Our State Fair
is a great State Fair.'

Suddenly going
all Rogers and Hammerstein,
swept up in some goofy gestalt.

The grass lushly green
from recent rains;
the sky
a limpid late-winter blue,
everything so perfectly technicolour.

Heads thrown back.
Young voices exultant.
Eyes focused ahead.
Keen laughter convulsing us.

'It only hurts when I laugh,'
I mug predictably to Lenore,
smiling adoringly back at me,
reaching for my hand.

Sonnet for Seventy-four

So, stumbling on in my guarded fashion,
I broach the month with pale and cautious eye.
Birthday milestones of a dying passion
and torn tapestries of a murky dye.
Once inflated with exhilaration,
piled high with games and books and sweets and toys,
I skirt low hollows in contemplation
of the retreat and rout of former joys.
Though southern Aprils are so beguiling –
No 'cruellest month' down here by any means –
in their undertow they're rarely smiling,
with crucifixion and invasion scenes:
A month when I face 'I am that I am…'
And enter the fool; then leave as a lamb.

Evening Coming On

Suddenly again
the long sadness.
Twilight seeping in –
a slate-grey tide.

Your dark tuft,
billowing that day
in the pool.
Cleft like bright abalone.

And after, still wet,
hugging the spotted
rocking-horse:
Its neck between your breasts.

A mad jockey ride,
laughing into the mane;
riding away,
riding, riding…

Gone.

Some Conclusions

(i)

Choose your partner
from a whirr of faces.
In the propulsive dance
of lust and death
you cannot be a wall-flower.

(ii)

Hoping to end things
on a happier note,
the joke escaped me,
laughing hysterically
on up the street.

(iii)

The silence grew
to immense proportions.
Everyone stopped to listen.
No one breathed
a word.

(iv)

The last bird,
a minute blackened thing,
stood by the generator,
too small and constipated
to lay its egg.

The Future

Sated now by me and mine,
the sun dips down below the line.

Those scattered friends, with whom I fought.
Those lost relations, yielding naught.

Busted, bruised, yet still abreast
of loved ones who have stood the test…

A body firm, though battle-scarred.
This weathered face: a lined postcard.

A mind that rambles through the pass
and gathers dew-drops in the grass.

For that is just the way it goes –
weighing words and counting crows…

And hopes, though battered, somehow bright,
with plans still dawning round midnight.

A spirit scoured; a soul unskinned
and fortunes written on the wind.

Each day engendered, leaved in brown;
each golden moment counted down.

Companions stroll beside me still;
their echoes cheerful through the chill.

And rutted roads wind on ahead
to rooms un-entered; books unread.

Last Dance

And so we dance:
Awkwardly,
tentatively on the debris;
feet slipping
on unsettled fragments,
shifting beneath us.

Dark shapes of friends,
undulating cautiously,
illumined by yellow lights
from opened doors.
Dual radios playing
like a stereo
from the old cars
drawn up,
a guard of honour,
diagonally at each side.

And so, on we dance:
'Solid Rock' morphing
into 'More Than This'…
Dancing close
with sweet Lorraine.
Robert and Lea
dancing closer,
stumbling on the rubble
of this Mountain of Love –
on the detritus
left by the Deens
up on Blueberry Hill.

A ring
of sudden ruination,
more treacherous now
than any sprung floor.

And, as we dance,
the wavering torch beams
closing in.
The bark of guards
and dogs:
Loud yelps and commands.

And we falter in our tableau.
We freeze in their spotlights…

But then, sweeping in
like a cloudburst
this Brisbane night,
Joan Jett and the Blackhearts:
'Crimson and Clover'
breaking over us all,
disarming mad dogs and men,
washing over
this pulverised concrete,
over and over,
to save the last dance,
the very last dance at Cloudland,
exclusively for us.

Are poems supposed
to just sit there
on the page?

Aren't they supposed
to get up
and dance?

www.ingramcontent.com/pod-product-compliance
Lightning Source LLC
Chambersburg PA
CBHW070101120526
44589CB00033B/1265